piano • vocal • guitar

best of
Jane Monheit

Cover photo by Lynn Goldsmith

ISBN 0-634-07011-8

CORPORATION

7777 W. BLUEMOUND RD. P.O. BOX 13819 MILWAUKEE, WI 53213

Visit Hal Leonard Online at
www.halleonard.com

Photo by Allan Titmuss

best of JANE Monheit

Contents

Biography

Jane Monheit has created an international sensation in jazz since she burst onto the scene singing in the 1998 Thelonious Monk Competition, and was quickly signed by manager Mary Ann Topper of the Jazz Tree.

The daughter of musicians, Jane learned that she had perfect pitch when she was a little girl and already a passionate fan of Ella Fitzgerald. After high school, she entered the Manhattan School of Music, where she became a student of Peter Eldridge, the singer/arranger and one of the founding members of the New York Voices. Monheit was singing in New York clubs while she was still a student, but it was her memorable performance in the Monk Competition that was her initial career breakthrough.

She recorded her first album, *Never Never Land*, in the company of legendary jazz veterans including pianist Kenny Barron, bassist Ron Carter, saxophonists David "Fathead" Newman and Hank Crawford. The album spent over a year in *Billboard's* Top Ten Jazz Albums list and was named "Best Recording Debut" by the Jazz Journalists Association. Her follow-up album, *Come Dream with Me*, debuted at #1 on the *Billboard* Jazz Chart in May of 2001. *In the Sun*, Monheit's third album, builds upon the reputation that Monheit has created to date as one of the strongest and most accomplished of the new voices in jazz. In addition to winning raves for her first three albums, she has wowed audiences and critics alike with her live performances around the world with her touring quartet.

Jane was recently signed to the Sony Classical label and will release her first album for them in September of 2004.

Photo by Jimmy Katz

Photo by Allan Titmuss

Photo by Bruce Moore

CHEEK TO CHEEK

from the RKO Radio Motion Picture TOP HAT

Words and Music by
IRVING BERLIN

Heav - en, _____ I'm in Heav - en. _____ And my

heart beats so that I can hard - ly speak. _____ And I

DETOUR AHEAD

By HERB ELLIS,
JOHN FRIGO and LOU CARTER

Smooth road,
Instrumental solo

clear day; why am I the on-ly one trav-'lin' this way?

CHEGA DE SAUDADE
(No More Blues)

English Lyric by JON HENDRICKS and JESSIE CAVANAUGH
Original Text by VINICIUS DE MORAES
Music by ANTONIO CARLOS JOBIM

HAUNTED HEART

Word by HOWARD DIETZ
Music by ARTHUR SCHWARTZ

HIT THE ROAD TO DREAMLAND

from the Paramount Picture STAR SPANGLED RHYTHM

Words by JOHNNY MERCER
Music by HAROLD ARLEN

*Chord Names For Guitar

I GOT IT BAD AND THAT AIN'T GOOD

Words by PAUL FRANCIS WEBSTER
Music by DUKE ELLINGTON

NEVER LET ME GO
from the Paramount Picture THE SCARLET HOUR

Words and Music by JAY LIVINGSTON
and RAY EVANS

I'M THRU WITH LOVE

Words by GUS KAHN
Music by MATT MALNECK and FUD LIVINGSTON

IT NEVER ENTERED MY MIND

from HIGHER AND HIGHER

Words by LORENZ HART
Music by RICHARD RODGERS

NEVER NEVER LAND

from PETER PAN

Lyric by BETTY COMDEN and ADOLPH GREEN
Music by JULE STYNE

ONCE I WALKED IN THE SUN

Words and Music by WILL JENNINGS,
IVAN LINS and CELSO VIAFORA

- til my life ___ is done. ___

SOMETHING TO LIVE FOR

Words and Music by DUKE ELLINGTON
and BILLY STRAYHORN

Moderately, freely

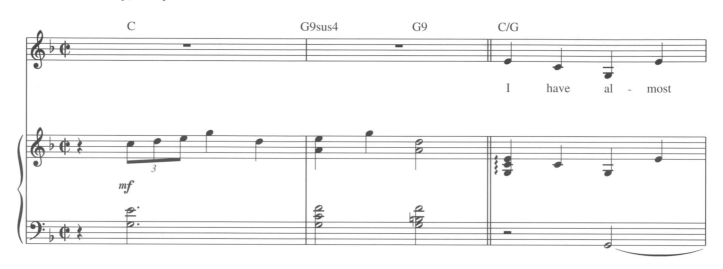

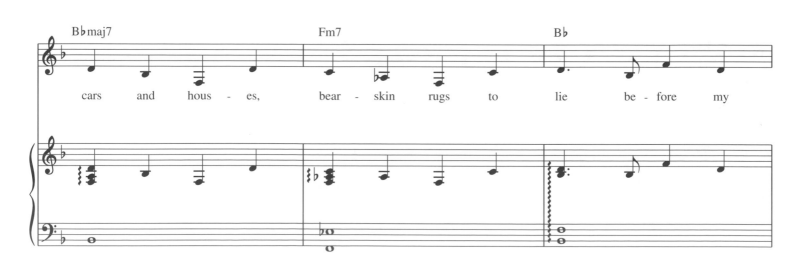